Other Works by Jack Fritscher

Novels

Some Dance to Remember
The Geography of Women
What They Did to the Kid
Leather Blues

Short Fiction

Rainbow County
Corporal in Charge of Taking Care of Captain O'Malley
Stand by You Man
Titanic
Stonewall: Stories of Gay Liberation
Sweet Embraceable You: Coffee House Stories

Non-Fiction

Gay San Francisco: Eyewitness Drummer
Gay San Francisco: Gay Pioneers
Mapplethorpe: Assault with a Deadly Camera
Popular Witchcraft
Love and Death in Tennessee Williams
When Malory Met Arthur: Camelot

www.JackFritscher.com

Television Today

A Primer of Critical Thinking, Censorship, Social Justice, and Fake News in American Popular Culture

Jack Fritscher, Ph.D.

Palm Drive Publishing
Sebastopol CA

©1971, 2020 Jack Fritscher, Ph.D.

All rights reserved.

Except for brief passages, no part of this book may be reproduced, stored in or introduced in a retrieval system, or transmitted in any form without the prior written permission of the copyright owner.

Previously published by Claretian Publications of Chicago; Editors: Mark J. Brummel, C.M.F., R.J. Liskowski, Tom Hogan; and Kevin Axe; February 1971; Volume 26, No. 2

Cover and book design: Mark Hemry

Published by Palm Drive Publishing, Sebastopol CA
Email: publisher@PalmDrivePublishing.com

Library of Congress Control Number: 2020934558

Fritscher, Jack 1939–

p.cm
ISBN   978-1-890834-47-0 print
          978-1-890834-48-7 ebook

1. Popular Culture 2. Critical Thinking 3. Media 4. Censorship
5. Television 6. Advertising 7. Gender 8. Social Justice

First Printing 2020
10 9 8 7 6 5 4 3 2
Palm Drive Publishing, Sebastopol CA
www.PalmDrivePublishing.com

For Kevin Axe, Frank Olson,
and Mark Hemry
who each made this book possible.

Epigraph

But in spite of his knowledge of many separate facts, the Captain never in his life had had an idea in his head. For the formation of an idea involves the fusion of two or more known facts. And this the Captain had not the courage to do.
   —Carson McCullers, *Reflections in a Golden Eye*

Contents

Stay Tuned! Television Today and 50 Years Ago xi
Reflections in a Golden Eye 1
Afternoon at the Soap Opera 19
TV's Queasy Kid Stuff. 27
Americanned Creativity 33
Old Stereotypes New Myths 53
Study Guide for Classroom Discussion. 67

STAY TUNED! TELEVISION TODAY AND 50 YEARS AGO

Principles of Critical Thinking Taught to Each Generation (Fake News Never Dies)

This book, written in 1970 when a pre-Watergate Richard Nixon was president, and republished during the 2020 occupation of the White House by Donald Trump, affirms that timeless principles of critical thinking do not change, nor does human behavior.

The necessity of critical thinking never goes away.

The goal for a person's liberation from authoritarianism through education is the ability to interpret, understand, and survive the towering babble of people, media, politics, religion, art, and society.

In the 1960s, universities were the crucible of revolution and change.

That so angered conservative politicians that they have continued to today to systematically de-fund education from kindergarten to college because citizens schooled in critical thinking are a population of resistance and change that threatens their riches, religion, rule, and reasoning.

I wrote this book while teaching American literature on one of those progressive university campuses in the 1960s when film-crazy and politically active students enthusiastically diverted arts-and-ideas discussions of classic novels into discussions of current film and media.

They impelled me to reinvent my "Literary Interpretation" class by adding film/television as a fourth genre to fiction, poetry, and drama as a relevant way to teach principles of critical thinking freshened via the popular culture of movie and television screens.

In the half-century since, the names of people and titles of programs have changed, but the principles of critical thinking remain the same.

All of human life ends up on television.

My thanks continue through the years to Kevin Axe, acquisitions editor for the *Today* magazine, run by the still thriving Claretian Publications of Chicago, which in 1966 published my feature article, "What to Do at a 'Dirty' Movie," aimed at helping traditional movie-goers interpret the value of the frank new art films of the 1960s.

Kevin and I had met as teenagers attending the same high school in the 1950s. In 1970, he commissioned my proposal for this book stylized for high-school students and teachers wanting to learn how to interpret the new dialogue, images, stereotypes, and archetypes in our media-saturated culture.

My thanks also to publisher Mark J. Brummel, C.M.F., editors R. J. Liskowski and Tom Hogan, and art director Ron Bean whose youthful design reflected the Pop Art of the 1960s. It was an honor they chose this to be the first issue of *Today* written by one author: *Television Today*, Volume 26, No. 2, February 1971.

—Jack Fritscher, 2020

REFLECTIONS IN A GOLDEN EYE

You are your one and only original critic.

Some Principles for Television, the 4th Genre;
for Censorship; for TV Politics;
and for the Revolution of Yourself

The dark ages ended twice as long ago as most of you are old. Vladimir Zworykin and Philo Farnsworth, the fathers of television, said *Let There Be TV* and there was TV. The world's age-old Age of Darkness ended when the first TV camera first beamed light into the first cathode receiver in the 1930s. Soon America had more to do than sit bored in brightly lighted living rooms knitting huge slipcovers for the Empire State Building. Suddenly there was TV and the people found it good.

TV, more than any other technology, has revolutionized our American heads. Nothing is anymore the same. As soon as the gas-wheel and the jet-wing extended our foot, we escaped our age-old imprisonment in time and geography. The telephone extended our ears and our voices. The TV camera externalized our sight. No longer are we imprisoned by the physics of how far we can hear, of how loud we can shout, or of how limited is our horizon.

Technology has amplified us. And freed us. TV technology especially has broken our isolation. But many people kick and scream and resist the 20th century. They resent losing the security of being left nicely alone on a remote farm or in an urban apartment. The concept of Man in Society, they blubber, is much more complicated and frightening than the concept of Man Alone. The Serpent brought trouble to Adam and Eve alone in Paradise. They ate themselves out of house and home, but the apple gave the two of them knowledge of good and evil. It gave them critical ability. Is TV the Eve who dares put us on the moon, into Asian jungles, campus disorders, and ghetto squalor?

Without TV, people could live comfortably isolated and unconcerned on Iowa farms, in Indiana villages, and in air-conditioned Chicago townhouses. The fact is, the Technological Revolution, far more than the Industrial Revolution, has forced us into contact with each other and each other's ideas and problems. TV has proved John Donne's and Thomas Merton's brother-keeping axiom: No man is an island.

Old ideas of time and space are dead, but old myths give rise to new. Time-honored styles of American living modulate into new fads and fashions. America celebrates, for better or for worse, the Now-ness of a Throw-Away Culture. Pity the citizens who can't or won't accept change as positive good.

Henry David Thoreau, America's first hip intellectual, said, in *Walden*, that: "Our inventions are wont to be pretty toys, which distract our attention from serious things.... We are in great haste to construct a magnetic telegraph from Maine to Texas; but Maine and Texas, it may be, have nothing important to communicate."

Technology can be no end in itself. What's the use of building television circuitry that webs the Earth's continents even up to the Moon, if television has nothing to say to the Earth and to the Moon? If, however, television does indeed find something to say to the Earth and the Moon and if you can't decipher it, what's the use of you watching your television?

* * * *

This is *Television Today*, the revolutionary electric TV coloring-book magazette.

But no more than you accept television, newspapers, or teachers as absolute truth can you accept this issue of *Today* about television as true. You are, in fact, your one and only original critic. You have to sift your sources. You won't like some of this issue and you don't have to accept any of it. What would you do if I sang out of tune? The fact of the matter is: this magazine issue, and these intellectual issues, are calculated to make you think, to make you more critical.

And criticism is no negative trip. Being critical is a positive act. Being critical is necessary if your head is to survive the onslaught of hemi-demi-semi truths and untruths that bang at your senses from television, radio, movies, books, periodicals, and other people. Being critical puts you on top. Criticism puts you in control. The critic exercises his own well-informed judgment. The responsibility is big; but the responsibility is no drag. Criticism is cross-examining *for yourself* the who, what, when, where, why, and how of a person, statement, art object, or situation.

Put The Beatles' "Revolution No. 9" on your record player. The Fab 4 sing carefully about the difference between revolution and evolution, about changing the world without destruction.

Revolution is change. Evolution is change. Notice how scientists constantly turn to animals for explanations of man's behavior? Once you accept evolution on a biological level (even if only as a theory where God intervened at a soul-point in time), you have to accept evolution on other levels as well: psychological evolution, social evolution, moral evolution. In the ninth century the Catholic Church owned slaves. Moral evolution occurred and the Church led Christianity's change to abolition. After World War II, Americans turned to the car as never before. Our society became mobile. This social evolution created our drive-in culture: restaurants; theatres; and, in California, drive-in mortuaries.

New England poet Robert Frost was a farmer as well as a poet and critic. He once said that we learn from our hands to our head. He meant he could not have written the poetic line "Something there is that doesn't love a wall" if he had not built stone-pile walls with his own raw hands, only to see the bitter New England winters work the rocks down. Frost meant literal hands make metaphorical heads.

A literal person calculates the distance and increasing velocity of a falling stone. A metaphorical person understands a rock whose roll reminds him of truths and insights into the human condition of life, love, and death. Frost meant you can't stop with arithmetic, which makes one equal a literal one. A man of critical insight understands how one appearance can signal two, three, or four hidden realities. Like getting a second and dirty meaning out of a first-level innocent joke.

Literal people view Ernest Hemingway's *The Old Man and the Sea* as a great ABC *Wide World of Sports* story about a fisherman whose oversized catch is attacked by sharks. Metaphorical people, who perceive the reality behind the fundamental appearance, see the literalist's one-to-one denotation that Hemingway's is a simple fish story; but they also see the metaphor, the connotation of one-to-two or one-to-three levels of reality—perhaps the story of the Old Man's catch is a universal statement about the human condition.

How many literal viewers watched Hemingway's story on TV (or read the book) and missed the metaphor: if you

TV Today

go for the big catch, chances are the sharks of life will try to tear you to shreds before you can bring it on home. Yet the try for Big Things, even failed Big Things, can be its own reward.

To get behind the literal level of meaning is not to reduce enjoyment of your TV watching. You actually increase it by giving it depth. 3-D TV is here. It's your mind that gives the flat screen its third dimension. Commercials, news, series, and specials all require your criticism. And your critical thinking, open-ended to new attitudes and new facts, can bring the Big Things home to the evolving and the new—if you have the Old Man's courage not to hide in your farm-and-townhouse isolation.

But, just because somebody has studied a lot or viewed every edition of CBS *Special Reports* doesn't mean he's developed his critical faculty. Listen to novelist Carson McCullers on her Army hero Captain Penderton:

> When he was a young lieutenant and a bachelor he had had much opportunity to read [and watch television].... His head was filled with statistics and information of scholarly exactitude. For instance, he could describe in detail the curious digestive apparatus of a lobster or the life history of a Trilobite. He spoke and wrote three languages gracefully. He knew something of astronomy and had read much poetry. [Here comes McCullers' good part!] But in spite of his knowledge of many *separate facts*, the Captain *never* in his life had *had an idea in his head*. For the formation of an idea involves the *fusion of two or more known facts*. And this the Captain had not the *courage* to do. (Italics added)

McCullers' novel is called *Reflections in a Golden Eye*. Think about it. TV—even in CBS' network symbol—is often termed a huge Eye. The screen reflects the room your television set sits in. It reflects the factual world the TV cameras transmit to it. And it reflects the attitudes of the popular commercial culture that sponsors it. Whether that TV Eye is "golden" or not depends not as much on the local and network programmers as it does on you the critical viewers who watch it.

* * * *

Television is the New World Literature, the fourth genre. The traditional genres of fiction, poetry, and drama pale by comparison to the impact of the TV omnibus. A classroom which teaches you only how to interpret stories and poetry is a classroom whose relevance was outdated when the last one-room schoolhouse folded its potbellied stove and its Port-O-San.

By the time the current "Imagineration" reaches kindergarten each child has spent one-fourth to one-half of his waking hours in front of the TV screen. By the time these children graduate from high school each one will have watched 15,000 hours of television. That is nearly 2,000 hours more time, as Senator Pastore points out, than he has spent in school. Only sleeping—certainly not reading or play-going—has required more time than his TV watching. Television has, in a sense, become the New Religion. It provides new icons, new totems, and new prophets for our society wandering in the desert of a cultural revolution.

In the womb-incubators of our warm TV sets, new myths proper to our times are shaped and formed. TV, in fact, has become the American medium equivalent to the process of canonization in the Catholic Church. No Broadway play, no novel, no Hollywood movie really makes it until the networks announce its sainting as a primetime series. Just so were Neil Simon's plays *The Odd Couple* and

Barefoot in the Park verified; just so was Grace Metalious' novel *Peyton Place* or William Faulkner's novel *The Long Hot Summer* realized; just so does a premiere on *Monday Night at the Movies* make real to a mass audience films that formerly played only to the patrons of limited seating in dark movie palaces.

Haskell Wexler's film about Chicago during Mayor Daley's 1968 Democratic Convention was called *Medium Cool*. The medium which moviemaker Wexler referred to was TV. He called it *cool* because TV, more than any other art form, can do everything to everybody. TV is *the* influential medium for man in a mass culture. So powerful is TV as informer and persuader that it sometimes finds itself cut down for its very virtues. Why is TV banned from our American courtrooms? Would our society be better for watching late night videotapes (to keep children from exposure) of the trial of the Chicago Seven? Of Charles Manson? Of Lieutenant Calley? Is it a moot question why TV was daily hassled out of the Chicago Democratic convention? Perhaps the answer lies somewhere in the Yippie street chant, "The whole world is watching." In free-speech and free-press America can there be people who wish to turn off the TV cameras? Who wish not to show us the agony of Cesar Chavez? Who wish to devolve us back into the Dark Ages where injustice and information were kept from the unwatching eyes of the world?

Whether or not you agree with the media freaks—hippies, yippies, or dippies—the point is that TV in the summer of 1968 made Chicago everybody's neighborhood. Since TV was let be, the whole world has lived on the same block. But should TV try to create us in its own image and likeness? Are we to believe, to buy, and to wear whatsoever TV commands?

* * * *

If we are to be more than a nation of sheep, we must be creatively critical of the dictates TV hands us. In the balance between *facts* and *attitudes*, TV more than any other contemporary medium tells us the facts we need to know about Washington D.C., Vietnam, pollution, and Jackie's Rich Greek. Unless we are as literally factual as Captain Penderton hiding out in his study, we ourselves have got to get together our *idea-attitudes* toward those simple separate *facts* that TV likes to sock to us.

Vice-President Spiro T. Agnew added Overton Taylor, emeritus professor at Harvard, and S.I. Hayakawa to his discussion of TV as attitude-maker. Agnew's Taylor says that television commercials have filled the minds of the young

> with pictures of fatuous, silly, blithely unconcerned well-to-do Americans as consumers, interested only in acquiring and enjoying trivial luxuries and pleasures, and oblivious to all the serious troubles of most people of their country and the world.

Agnew's Hayakawa declares:

> The world makes all sorts of demands the television set never told you about, such as study, patience, hard work, and a long apprenticeship in a trade or profession before you may enjoy what the world has to offer.

Agnew himself wrote in *TV Guide*:

> How much of the terrible impatience of so many young people—evident in the virulence of their protests—can be traced to the disparity between the real world and that Epicurean world inside the television set where the proper combination of pills and cars and cigarettes and deodorants can bring relief

from suffering and instant gratification of all their material wants and desires?

Henry Steele Commager, quoted by Agnew, wrote:

> On the whole the contribution of this new and potentially great medium of television to education… is meager, and is more than counterbalanced by its contributions to noneducation and to the narrowing of intellectual horizons. Television…neither transmits the knowledge of the past to the next generation, nor contributes to professional training, nor does it expand the boundaries of knowledge.

Such a collage of attitudes about attitudes indicates that the American Establishment is having no love affair with Lady Television. It can't abide her trend-setting changes. Agnew has asked, "How much disorder, how many of these illegal demonstrations which pockmark the country would ever take place if the ever-present television camera were not there?"

Militantly anti-establishment, Yippie leader Abbie Hoffman views TV as the prime instrument of radicalization, the prime instrument of revolutionary attitudes.

(Are Mr. Agnew and Mr. Hoffman in that much agreement after all?)

Another of the Chicago Seven said openly: "Our real goal has been to get this trial on television." Hoffman himself has repeated time and again the importance of TV as an educative medium: "We no longer need the schools. What we need to do is to give everybody a TV set. You can learn everything you need to know from TV."

With such divergent views, you are left to your own critical devices.

Television, the Ultimate American Invention, is like America: neither as bad nor as good as either extreme would name it. Nicholas Johnson, FCC Commissioner, has said of America: "This country is a great experiment. For close to 200 years we have been testing whether it is possible for an educated and informed people to govern themselves."

Those right-wing and left-wing Americans who both claim to have the absolute (and opposite) answers for America seem to forget our Experimental Status. Absolute dictates are so far from the real American temper that we are the only nation in the world whose National Anthem begins and ends with a question.

Ralph Waldo Emerson in his essay "The American Scholar" defined the dubious role of the All-American Critic in this way: The intellectual is simply Man Thinking.

By Emerson's definition you are the American intellectuals as you criticize the role TV plays in the American experiment. Your sheer attendance at an institution of higher learning gives objective verification that if you are not the intellectuals of America, no one is.

People Thinking ought to be able to judge for themselves. Yet NBC President Julian Goodman frankly admits that American television, because it is the informer, "is now under threat of restriction and control." CBS President Frank Stanton states that "attempts are being made to block us." ABC News Chief Elmer Lower predicts that television may "face the prospect of some form of censorship."

NBC, CBS, and ABC, more impactful than the two wire services of the Associated Press and the United Press International, inform America of what there is to know. Thomas Jefferson, aware of England's tyrannical censorship, said, "The way to prevent error is to give the people full information of their affairs." Tom must be revolving in his grave, for recently:

- Censors have cut actor Robert Montgomery off the NBC *Tonight Show* when he mentioned a certain CBS station under FCC investigation.

- Unnamed powers-that-be have caused the networks to tie up Truman Capote's documentary special *Death Row: USA*, so that not even National Educational Television (NET) can show the shocking brutalities Capote has unearthed in the American Way of Capital Punishment. A Supreme Court ruling seems in the offing.

- Censors have scissored Joan Baez' anti-draft views from the CBS *Smothers Brothers*. Eventually the whole award-winning *Smothers Brothers Comedy Hour* was silenced.

- Authorities, like the fabled "Priscilla Goodbody" of NBC, have not permitted Ralph Nader or Christine Jorgensen on any NBC talk shows. Crusader Nader, author of the anti-Detroit book *Unsafe at Any Speed*, is a consumer-protector who often attacks products that happen to be the networks' major accounts. (Auto advertising runs about four-hundred million dollars annually.) Miss Jorgensen some years ago sustained transsexual surgery. The censors, despite best-selling books, popular movies, and daily newspaper accounts, judge the TV audience too immature to deal with the subject.

- NBC—perhaps protecting its Christian sponsors and viewers—denied Johnny Carson permission to feature a seance on his Halloween *Tonight Show*, although Witchcraft Churches are now protected under the freedom-of-religion clause of the United States Constitution.

- Censors have ordered cuts in most recent Hollywood films to make them suitable for TV. *Secret Ceremony*, a terrible flop starring Elizabeth Taylor and Mia Farrow, not only had to be cut, but certain scenes left out of the original theater print had to be edited back into the TV print. Whoever these censors are, adding and subtracting footage, they obviously want everything their way with little discrimination left up to the individual viewer.

Local stations, disagreeing with their parent network, often announce that "We reserve the right to delay network programming for showing at a more convenient time." The "convenient time" for showing *Bill Cosby* and *Julia* on many Southern TV stations never comes—for obvious reasons. More absurdly, at least one TV station (WMAA-TV) in Jackson, Mississippi—where education has long been so wretched it needs all the help it can get—refuses to air *Sesame Street* because of the integrated cast. Surely that's the censor cutting off his racist nose to spite his children's minds.

If you doubt this subtle suasion of vested interests, note well the FCC's expose that NBC anchorman Chet Huntley was in his newscasts "editorializing *against* the Wholesome Meat Act at a time when he and his business partners were heavy investors in the cattle and meat business."

Don't think it wasn't a major triumph against moneyed censorship when the Supreme Court forced TV to run the American Cancer Society's cautions against cigarette smoking. The networks resisted because the Cancer Crusade led—as they suspected it would—to the banning of all cigarette commercials, in order to protect the impressionable young. Consider that in 1970 the tobacco companies sold nine billion dollars worth of cigarettes, and provided TV with its largest single source of advertising revenue.

* * * *

Okay. TV is a mind-bender. So whom do you trust? The censors? The professional critics hired by *Life*, *Look*, and *TV*

Guide? The businessmen? Yourself? The FCC's Nicholas Johnson (in *TV Guide*) argues for open TV in a free society:

> I would far rather leave the heady responsibility for the inventory in America's "marketplace of ideas" to talented and uncensored *individuals*—creative writers, performers and journalists from all sections of this great country—than to the *committees* of frightened financiers in New York City. Wouldn't you? I think so.

Johnson does not mean that children should not be protected from certain scenes and subjects. They should. But that protection ought to be descriptive censorship, not prescriptive.

Descriptive censorship is advisory. It reviews taped programs and films, recommending the level of audience suitability. Parents for their children, or individuals for themselves, can then decide to view or not to view. The important point is that the choice remains with the informed and free individual.

Prescriptive censorship, on the other hand, autocratically announces that no one may watch a show. The individual viewer has no choice since the network and/or its affiliate station snatches free choice from his hands and either edits or never airs the program. Our American Motion Picture Ratings (GP, M, R, X) are advisorily descriptive. Hitler's bookburning censorship was prescriptive.

Someone once predicted that we will one day have Fascism in America, but we will call it Americanism. When people start managing our news, when people start prescriptive censorship, we are halfway there. If the right-or-left-wing rumblings of this poisoned kind of Americanism are among us, they will be heard first over TV. It will be the insatiable eye and ear of the TV camera that will first catch it and experience it for what it is. Free TV is the stand where free America lives or dies. TV is the thermometer of our times. Like Chicken Man, it's everywhere. To find out how fevered we are as a nation, turn on the TV and tune in the popular temperature.

Even if political suppression of TV is not this much of a radical danger, then consider the basis of the two alternatives of censorship.

Prescriptive censorship is insulting. It is predicated on the assumption that people are essentially stupid and uncritical. It would dismiss democracy as the glorification of the lowest common denominator. Descriptive censorship, however, is really no censorship at all, predicating itself on the critical thinking and awareness of the intelligent viewer. It terms democracy a climate where freedom of responsible choice is available to the informed mind.

A sub-classification of descriptive censorship is the Natural Censorship of the Hour in Primetime. This means that adult programming, unsuitable for children, can be telecast after ten p.m. Presumably, impressionable youngsters are bedded down by that hour. Why, indeed, should our entire evening programming be censored to the twelve-year-old level when the twelve-year-olds are not watching? Must TV, like so much else in American culture, be child-oriented rather than adult-oriented? Once the nation accepts the ten p.m. to midnight slot as an adult viewing time, TV can do away with much of the nonsense that TV's chief censor, Stockton Helffrich, the director of the National Association of Broadcasters Code Authority, tries to pull off at 485 Madison Avenue, New York. (And if *you* don't like what he tries to do, write him about it.)

A nation hardly praiseworthy for its censorship or its segregation, South Africa—as very few Americans realize—has no television at all. The openly racist South African government fears the educative power of TV on the Blacks who are kept in strict confinement and curfew. South Africa, obviously, has not abolished slavery. In order to keep their Black citizens "in their place," the apartheid South African government has prescriptively censored the entire medium of television from their country. Currently, for their 1971 elections, the liberal Opposition Party is running on a platform promoting television as an informative medium for all South Afrikaners, White and Black.

Of the two censorships, prescriptive and descriptive, it's not too hard to guess which the thinking American would jealously prefer.

* * * *

TV thrives on dramatic impact. Vice-President Agnew blames the television camera for young America's turn from political indifference to active involvement. He says:

> "Action" holds a viewing audience. Thus, there is competition among the network newsmen to pack "action" into their broadcasts. If one point of view is presented, a conscious effort is made to find its opposite and present a new controversy to the public. This raises the question: how much overemphasized controversy and contrived action can be presented night after night to the American people before reality is clouded...?

Is this a very high opinion of the critical ability of the average middle-American? Do audiences swallow tele-dramatics as uncritically as the Vice-President suggests when he says that young people

> enjoy confrontation because they were brought up on television instead of books. They're conditioned to action and emotion, not words. It is a perfectly

natural, everyday thing. They see action, violence, confrontation on television and they are naturally more conditioned to action than logic. The danger is that they tend to become caught up in the event....

Can our controversial Vice-President really mean what he's saying? The young "Imageneration," admittedly fascinated by the non-verbal psychedelia of sound and lightshows, has not read five hundred books to match the five hundred movies they've viewed for fun by high-school graduation. But does this mean that our main source of information should be prescripted? Does this mean that we should be denied the vision of television which extends us into alternative worlds and springs us out of the ghettoes of our minds? What would Thomas Jefferson say? Does Mr. Agnew really mean such a put-down of young Americans who are so socially aware and politically active that the voting age is just now being lowered to eighteen to match the drafting age? Can you accept the Vice-President any less critically than you accept Walter Cronkite or this very issue of *Today*?

At one time in American political history, time and geography tyrannized over our political system. Technology has removed that twin tyranny, but the antiquated political system remains. It no longer takes the presidential-election count from either Maine or Texas a full week to make it to the nation's capitol. TV-telephone-computer complexes can tabulate instantly in the District of Columbia how John Brown voted in Sebastopol, California. Technology has removed the tyranny, but the electoral college (designed by our Founding Fathers to counteract it) remains. The electoral college is a debate in itself. Whether it is a safeguard to the American system or not, from a sheer representational point of view of one vote per customer, the electoral college is now a pre-technological dinosaur. Contemplate this as your critical mind considers next year's presidential election.

Like it or not these days, we have Election by Television. The rich, who can afford the TV time, and the talented (especially former actors), who know how to relax into the medium, have in recent elections proven themselves winners. Sure, the ordinary guy can still run for high offices; but gone are the days when he could win. During the 1968 campaigns, candidates spent sixty million dollars on TV and radio advertising. This is high finance. No wonder that on local, state, and federal levels it is the wealthy who tend to be the candidates for offices of governor, senator, congressman, and president.

Wait! As of last summer, hope looms large for the candidate who was born in a log cabin and still lives there. Congress in 1970 passed a bill to effect a basic control of the political uses of television.

To even matters out between the Have and the Have-Not Candidates, Congress has ruled that each campaigner's budget will be limited to seven cents per voter in the last election. If ten people voted in last season's senatorial race, this season's candidate for senator can spend seventy cents.

Actually, seventy-three million people voted for the president in 1968. This limits the 1972 broadcast budget to 5.1 million dollars per party. Compare this to Humphrey's 7.1 million, and Nixon's 12.6 million in 1968. For campaigners in states with highly inflated campaign budgets like New York, 1972 will be a cheaper year. At the going rate of seven cents, the maximum allowed in 1972 in New York can total only ten to twenty percent of the total that New York campaigners blew on broadcasting in 1968. In addition, stations must give the lowest possible rates to all candidates, cutting last season's campaign fees from thirty-five to fifty percent.

Heavy stuff, all this.

But if this issue of *Today* doesn't confront the same world that TV has led you to live in, then this issue has not reached you where you live.

If it doesn't do that, then it can never reveal to you the worlds of life and love and activity behind and beyond the teleworld you know. If, after you've read it all and have subjected it to discussion and criticism, it still does nothing for you, then trash it under a landslide of not-so-soft psychedelia.

Gather critical acumen where ye may. It's not singing out of tune to say the intelligent are going to inherit the Earth. There is going to be no Street Revolution. At least none that will do any good. Like "April Come She Will," so will the soft but effective Abstract Revolution. Gather those changes. Take them with you into the existing systems. And, with well-aimed critical thinking, go out and revolutionize and change the institutions—from the inside out.

AFTERNOON AT THE SOAP OPERA

The Not-So-Secret Storm
"It's my party, and I'll cry if I want to."

The other afternoon I turned on the television. I hadn't viewed a TV serial for six weeks, not since the day I spent in CBS STUDIO 43, observing the rehearsals and taping of the most venerable of the Old Soaps, *The Secret Storm*. In the six weeks since I'd left New York, actress Mary Stuart had not stirred from her hospital bed. She was suffering from blindness (as temporary, never fear, as everything in the soap operas); and her fiancé was dead, I think, in South America. Mary should have known better than to languish in her hospital bed. Since she first appeared in the first episode of *The Secret Storm* seventeen years ago, things have always turned out best for stalwart Mary, Queen of Soaps.

Now understand, I'm not given to watching soap serials, except in late January when I get my annual bout of winter flu. Sometimes, however, I watch *Secret Storm* out of loyalty to my friend Frank Olson who is the show's lighting director. Frank lives in Manhattan, on 72nd Street, and if I cajole him enough when visiting the city, he can usually find a way to pass me through CBS' tight security. Frank knows agony when he sees it. And why not? The folks on *Secret Storm* have been tortured from head to toe for years.

"You can visit the set," Frank tells me, "but promise to stand clear. We work a tight schedule."

I promise, and the next morning I follow Frank down the long cream-colored corridors of CBS New York. He guides me through the Telecine Film center, past the cameras that send *Tuesday Night at the Movies* out across the prairies and mountains of America. Farther down the hall the news-editors monitor the competition of NBC and ABC. In a nearby glass room stands an empty desk waiting for Walter Cronkite to inform the nation. We pass through STUDIO 41 where Barbra Streisand filmed her first specials, where Ed Sullivan aired his shows before moving to his own Sullivan Theatre, where every four years Walter Cronkite and Harry Reasoner cover the National Elections.

In the *Secret Storm* Control Room, eleven technicians bend intently to their dials, their cue boards, and their screen monitors. The preview screen is lighted. In close-up, *Storm* star Stuart's face flashes on for a rehearsal take. Next to her black-and-white close-up, a color screen monitors what CBS viewers in Indiana and Illinois are watching at that moment on network television. A third screen is dark: when it lights, it will carry today's color-taping of *Secret Storm* which will be canned for telecast on the network tomorrow.

"In our half hour," Frank says, "we figure seven minutes of assorted opening titles, commercials, closings, and station breaks. Between our show and the next one comes a ninety-second break in the network for local station identification and local commercials. We tape about twenty-two minutes of plot a day. That may not seem much, but at five shows a week that's one hundred and ten minutes or the same as your average feature-length movie. You could say we film a movie a week."

Just then actress Joan Copeland, whose brother Arthur Miller wrote *Death of a Salesman*, walks through the Control Room. At night she understudies Katharine Hepburn's lead role in the hit Broadway musical *Coco*. By day, she plays a well-intentioned crazy lady who cries a lot over her ingrate daughter-in-law. She looks very elegant because today she gets to be happy for a change, sitting on a bench, talking to her son in a park full of plastic flowers and green plastic grass. (Her park looks natural on color TV, but in the studio it looks as tacky as a discount store display window.)

Frank and I follow Joan onto the soundstage. On the back of the gray flats someone has stenciled PERMANENT "SEARCH" SET CBS. On the other side, the flats resemble the walls of four different rooms, mostly doctors' offices and hospital rooms. Off to one side is the display-window plastic park.

Frank introduces me to Sidney Walters, the Stage Manager. Sidney is harried, but friendly. He has time for one more rehearsal before today's taping. Mary, who is currently "blind," keeps knocking a hospital bedpan to the cement floor. "You're not blind until the camera starts, Mary."

Mary smiles and rehearses her blind-bit again. The metal pan clangs to the floor, louder this time. Sidney takes it in stride. He decides to work the clumsy bedpan into the final shooting. It will increase sympathy for Mary's pathetic situation.

A cameraman dollies his Norelco CBS color camera past me toward Queen Mary. He accuses me of being a spy from NBC. He pressures his camera slightly with a finger and the huge machine responds smoothly with a quiet vertical rise.

"You're taking notes on this stuff?" Sidney says to me. He pretends no one could take *Secret Storm* seriously. But Sidney manages the floor with the tight aplomb of a professional. A stage manager rolls with the slick punches. There's a cool honesty in that.

Frank makes a last minute adjustment on one of the six hundred lights that blaze down on us. Mary mops a thin moustache of sweat from her upper lip. She looks tired of sitting in bed for two hours practicing her scene, waiting while Frank adjusts the lights perfectly for her.

The two other cameras roll in. They dolly easily over the gray cement floor. Black electrical cords, like inch-thick serpents, coil over the gray. The three cameramen wear ear-and-mouth microphones. They are older than the two boom-mike operators. One boomman is young and hip; the other is young and Black. Frank tells me they're both new to the show. They're talented and on their way up the technical side of TV production.

A woman dressed as a nurse says to a man costumed as a doctor, "Don't you feel a terrible draft in here, darling?"

Like many viewers, she has him confused with a real MD who, like Marcus Welby, can prescribe a cure for any situation. Sidney calls out: "Hold all the talking, please. Quiet."

A man with a teleprompter moves into Mary's hospital set. He stands slightly off camera. His yellow scroll unrolls in his machine. If she wanted, Mary could read her lines from his prompter. More often than not she has them memorized. (If at times your favorite soap actors bob their heads a lot while talking to each other, what they are doing is reading their own teleprompters over one another's shoulders.)

Mary's favorite doctor enters her scene. He is costumed for surgery. His gown, like her sheets, is tinted light blue. (White, because it glares, is rarely used in a color studio.) His make-up is perfect. Camera 3 shoots his entrance from the knees up. Good thing. On his feet are a comfortably scuffed pair of old house slippers. Mary is in the foreground.

Mary and Doctor Rogers whisper their lines. I am seven feet away and I can hardly hear a word. Unlike stage actors, they speak even lower than real conversation. The boom-mike hovers like a god over their intimacy, recording dialogue so simple even Tommy Smothers could understand it. "You have at least a twenty percent chance," the doctor says.

"Excuse me," the director's voice comes over a ceiling squawk box. He interrupts the rehearsal lines from the Control Room next door. "Excuse me. Give me a beat right before 'a twenty percent chance.'"

"You have at least," the doctor-actor pauses, "a twenty percent chance." The rehearsal continues, then breaks for lunch.

"How do you like the show?" Frank asks me in the commissary. "Okay," I say. We eat chipped beef on toast.

* * * *

But I feel less than okay. The soap opera is an anesthetized world.

As of January 1971, at least nineteen soap operas are telecast each day five days a week. That's ten hours daily and fifty hours weekly of a world completely separated from contemporary reality. How did this huge block of TV programming happen? People need escape, I know. But the soap opera is not escape; it is denial, masochistic, narcotic. If TV ever lies to us, it lies to us about our world in the afternoon.

The magnificent critic Marya Mannes, who happens to be a Catholic, points out this TV lie in *TV Guide*.

> I wager teenagers would stare with hooting disbelief at what passes for their kind on daytime serials. To be sure, the girls wear long hair and the boys longer hair than they used to, and, as I said, the plotline sooner or later includes some alienated youngster with a problem. But what of the new young breed of social and political activists, what of the young idealists and draft protesters who court contempt and prison for their passionate beliefs?

And what of the millions of city families living, or trying to live, through strike after strike, through hopeless traffic, through noise and pollution and crowds and the daily brutalities of life? ...What conceivable relation to this common reality do these neat serial shadows have?

Soap opera shows us day after day gleaming hospitals copiously staffed with impeccable doctors and charming nurses, but have they any relation to the critical shortages in our national health care, and to the crushing financial burden sickness places on the American citizen? Who do they think they are kidding—or conning?

What should I have said to Frank in the CBS commissary? That soaps can leave a dulling and distorting film? That might be suitable to Miss Mannes; but where I come from you don't smart-mouth your friends. Besides, Frank and Sidney and CBS don't make the programs. They only supply the demand.

But, if they don't make the programs, who does? In truth, you do. You are the program-maker when you stand in the check-out lane where you shop. TV programming, like democracy itself, can—unless properly disciplined—settle down to glorifying the lowest common denominator. If you object to TV being the new "opiate of the people," if you object through the right channels to the narcotizing irrelevance of the soaps or any other program, chances are you'll be heard. (If you approve of what you see, let your approval be known too.)

To lobby effectively, send one dollar to National Television Advertisers (NTA), 3245 Wisconsin Avenue, Berwyn, Illinois, 60402. NTA will return to you the addresses and names of five hundred company presidents who sponsor TV programming. Tell the soap company presidents that you want to see their sponsored programs as relevant to our times as are their pollution-conscious commercials.

Secondly, write, don't telephone, the manager of your local TV station. In your letter, state clearly your objection or your praise and include a copy of the letter you have sent to the local and national sponsors who keep that manager's station on the air.

The fate (so far) of the honest sudser has been interesting. In 1968, the BBC super-soaper *The Forsyte Saga* so mesmerized England, Scotland, and Wales that the churches moved the Sunday Vesper services back an hour. By 1971, however, no one of the Big Three American Networks dared telecast this critically and popularly acclaimed Continuing Story (as *Peyton Place* used to be billed). Only the courageous NET (National Educational Television) has shown *The Forsyte Saga*, and then—because of its limited network resources—only at odd hours, locally, and without nationwide coverage. Consider this. NET's daring series, *Bird of an Iron Feather*, a Continuing Story of ghetto Blacks, has hardly become a household word. *Bird* was roundly condemned in Chicago and elsewhere because it used unpretty ghetto situations and profane ghetto language. *Forsyte* tells it like it was. *Bird*, with a Ford Foundation grant, tells it like it is. *Secret Storm* tells it phoney.

Could it be we don't want TV to tell the truth? Could it be that we want TV only to narcotize us, to drug us into false tranquillity? If that is so, then TV should be as outlawed as heroin.

* * * *

Back in *The Secret Storm* studio, the organist glissands down the keyboard warming up the background music for the day's taping. On SET 1, Mary Stuart crawls back into bed. On SET 5, Joan Copeland sits cheerily in her plastic park, hoping—I suppose—she can sing *Coco* on Broadway tonight.

Sidney waits as Frank cues one last spotlight. He calls for quiet.

The three cameras roll.

The mikes boom in.

Mary whispers her lines.

Her metal bedpan crashes to the floor.

They're professionals, all of them. They can't understand why a person from the real world would spend the day on their set. In their minds, the public has asked them for "reel" reality not "real" reality.

Earlier, Frank told me, "By union rules, we have to roll full credits at least once a week. So on days, when we're a little short of storytime, we fill in with extra credits of the entire cast and crew."

Credit must, after all, be given where credit is due. And the Afternoon Wasteland of Time and Talent is mostly the fault of the viewer who is easily satisfied when *Dark Shadows* causes *The Edge of Night* to dim not only *The Guiding Light*, but *The Best of Everything*.

Even with loyalty to Frank, I think I'll not watch *The Secret Storm* for another six weeks.

Will Mary-of-the-crashing-bedpan still be blind?

Probably.

TV'S QUEASY KID STUFF

SESAME STREET

Try on a parent's point of view and see if you can make it through the Saturday AM teleworld.

By the time today's child hits kindergarten, he's logged 3,000 hours of TV. He'll watch 12,000 more hours before he graduates from high school. So how can a parent be surprised when his three-year-old toddles in reciting the "Pledge of Allegiance"? Who taught him *that*? TV taught him that. And plenty more.

BANG! You're dead!

TV creates the American child's world.

Preschoolers watch weekday cartoons from nine to ten a.m. and grade-schoolers are programmed from 3:30 to six p.m. Besides the daily programming of the local *Romper Room* aired daily with Miss Nancy by local stations, the network series, *Captain Kangaroo*, and the independent series, *Sesame Street*, kids get it socked to them the hardest on Saturday mornings. And some of the socking could be hazardous to their health.

The Monkees rock 'n' roll series reruns daytimes to great applause. Their style, patterned after the early Beatles films, has filtered down the last few seasons from the teenybopper to the bubblegummer. (*Bubblegummer* is the name business has for the preschoolers who not only have their own money, but also influence what their parents buy.)

When *The Monkees* fast-pace crosses with *Laugh-In*'s quick episodes, the kids get something excellent: *Sesame Street*.

If today's preschooler isn't watching *Sesame*, he'll be behind his kindergarten competition. To augment Project Headstart, two National Councils, of Negro and of Jewish Women, have promoted the *Sesame* series in the ghettoes. VISTA workers have organized viewing groups. RCA and other corporations have donated over two hundred *Television-Sets-for-Sesame*. *Sesame* opens the child.

Sesame Street is ultimate TV. It uses image *and* sound. Turn off the picture and the child can't follow the show any more than you can follow the action of a pictureless *Mission: Impossible* that never has much dialogue. For contrast, turn off *Bonanza*'s or *Disney*'s picture; the ear still follows the plot. Until recently most TV shows have been no more than old radio shows glorified with electronic images.

Sesame Street has caught the commercial network executives up short. The network moguls have most often limited children's programs to old cartoons, an occasional *Heidi*, and a 2.5 million dollar budget for *Captain Kangaroo*. Little did they care about program quality as long as the commercials tricked the kids into nagging their parents to buy certain cereals, certain soaps, and certain toys.

Suddenly, *Sesame Street* with eight million dollars (half from private foundations and half from Federal funds) re-imagined TV's successfully slick commercial sell. *Sesame* creator Joan Cooney now "sells" the alphabet, and counting, and the differences between squares, triangles, and rectangles to two through five-year-olds on three hundred stations. *Sesame* thus sets the record for the largest exposure ever of any regular series. That makes those TV moneymen blanch a bit. Coming soon? A second *Sesame* series for seven to ten-year-olds with emphasis on reading skills.

Repetition is the key to education. *Sesame*'s repetition of image and sound is its essence. Adults may find repetition a bore, but kids (in the age group who like to have the same bedtime story repeated nightly) don't. They groove and improve on it. They like the familiar mixture of puppets, drawings, films, games, animals, and especially conversations.

Sesame is one program that knows kids. And respects them. It doesn't condescend. Its psyching is right on the beam. This year's first-grade teachers had to adjust their attitudes, curriculum, and methods to the *Sesame* Generation.

The best art supposedly conceals its art. *Sesame Street* has far more form than is apparent. Each program is carefully divided into five segments, with each segment repeated in various forms throughout the sixty-minute barrage.

Sesame Street, Episode 119 was structured as follows:

> 1. LETTERS: I, P, U. Jackie Robinson recites the alphabet. The hidden attitude is that black men can be intellectual leaders and lose none of their cool masculinity.
> 2. NUMBERS: 8, 9. The concept of quantity.
> 3. EMOTIONS: The child learns how to act out and understand his inner feelings and tensions.
> 4. CONCEPTS: The idea of *more* in comparison to the idea of *less*; points of view (teaches development of the critical ability to reason and distinguish).
> 5. SONG: "Counting." (Often stories or films are substituted.)

If ever TV had one, *Sesame Street* is a real variety show.

* * * *

The best of Saturday programs is *The Banana Splits* and *H. R. Pufnstuf*. *Pufnstuf* stars fifteen-year-old British actor, Jack Wild, an Oscar-nominee for *Oliver*. From an adult point of view, *Pufnstuf* is easier to take. It's a kind of a mod *Wizard of Oz* which mixes musical numbers with bell-bottoms, and amusing humans with friendly gremlins.

The Banana Splits is part of the Hanna-Barbera Animation Empire. If Disney dominates theatre films, HB rules the telescreens. Hanna-Barbera left the Hollywood studios in the early sixties to launch their own *Huckleberry Hound*. Huck and his friends now run the world of Bubblegum. Their mixture of cartoons like *Hillbilly Bears* and live-action series like *Danger Island* is a notch or two above some other cartoons like *Heckle and Jeckle, Tom Slick*, and *George of the Jungle*. In these shows some very strange attitudes affect the child.

Much TV has a sad morality.

Where *Sesame Street* emphasizes songs about "What Fathers Do," many kid-shows portray "Daddy as a Dummy." Hardly better than Jackie Gleason's *The Honeymooners* (which provides the plots for *The Flintstones*) many children's shows use the same "Dagwood Syndrome" that has marred adult sitcoms for years. Does exposing children to stupid TV males and spineless fathers alter their respect for paternal intellect and authority? Can they admire only the violently strong super-heroes like *Spider Man* or *The Super 6*?

A second sad thing to catch Saturday mornings—besides the violence—is the absence of women. *Clutch Cargo* wouldn't know what to do with a lady. When, however, a woman is present, she is either dizzy and helpless, like Penelope Pittstop, or comically evil like Witchy-Poo on *Pufnstuf* or Sabrina's aunt on *The Archie Show*. It's very difficult for a little girl to learn from TV what her role as a woman will one day be.

Don't make a judgment, however, until you sit down two or three Saturdays and catch the Bubblegum teleworld. Like it or not, this is what the kids see. We can't deny them the TV; there's too much good to be learned from it. We can BIFF BAM POW watch their programs and try to straighten out in conversation what we find faulty or plain wrong. We can creatively take the occasion to hone the beginning of the critical thinking faculties they'll need to make it through the media-crush of contemporary electronic life.

Censorship, it bears repeating, is a delicate thing.

Turning off the set makes it attractive forbidden fruit. Turning off won't do. The creative and open-minded parent (or older brother and sister) knows what the children are seeing and uses that exposure as a stepping stone to reinforce the good and explain the dubious.

The creative parent uses the controversial program to start a conversation with his child. Through communication comes mutual understanding. Watch the kids' shows and learn about the kids' world. They have no choice but to live in it. They need non-uptight adults to show them how to cope with divergent concepts.

Adults have the choice of understanding this new "Imageneration"—or not.

Wise are the parents these days who have discussions with their kids from infancy on up.

Conversation is what friends have, right?

AMERICANNED CREATIVITY

Advertising brainwashes our facts and our attitudes toward facts.

How the medium gets into you and how to get into the medium.

Those were the days, my friend. She came on all sweetness and light. Wholesome. Long summer dress. Long hair. Big summer hat. A change, man. Like lightning in her eyes. She whipped off her innocence with her straw hat. She belted: "Yeooo…can take Salem out of the country, BUT."

Can you, can any of you, resist adding: "You can't take the country out of Salem."

Of course not.

Until this Sweet Young Belter and the Marlboro Man were, along with all cigarette commercials, dropped from the telewaves, no one could resist saying Salem's name. Even non-smokers soaked up the brainwash.

Every ad agency aims to make you say its product's name. To say the name of the brand is to burn it into your brain. In the land of the free, we are programmed by TV advertising.

TV can make you want what you never knew you wanted. Blacks in Watts watch TV and want the same Good Life that Evanston Whites can buy. A pretty girl with curly brown hair watches a Clairol commercial. Right off, she wants the straight blonde Surfer Girl Look.

But, what if society keeps Blacks from buying the life that TV promises? What if that brown-haired girl doesn't have more fun as a blonde? Was the radical Abbie Hoffman right, after all, to say that every American can learn all he needs to know from TV? How to keep teeth bright, toilets clean, and underarms sweet.

So who needs Salem, Clairol, and Abbie Hoffman's boring old Revolution?

You do.

At least, you and your critical self-defense can't ignore them. The reason you can't is that, like Mount Everest, they are there. And if mountaineers climb Everest simply "because it's there," then we scale the TV pitch because it, too, is there. And like some roaring avalanche down Everest's slopes, what is there, affects us.

Remember this commercial? "Come to where the flavor is, come to...? Chances are, you do. You can hardly help saying "Marlboro Country."

Don't let it swell your ego though. Programmed chickens can peck out "Raindrops Keep Falling on My Head," if they get enough corn for their reward. Did you have any choice *not* to learn commercial jingles? Not if you turned on the TV, you didn't. *Repetitio est mater studiorum* they used to say in Latin class. Loosely translated that means: Repetition is the mother of studies. Repeat anything often enough and it will stick.

* * * *

Once upon an American time, TV advertisers watched a motion-picture experiment. In 1958, the producers of *My World Dies Screaming* tried to increase the shock of their horror movie. They knew that the human eye sees "motion" at basically twenty-four still frames per second in 16 millimeter. With this physiological fact in mind, they calculated that if they flashed the word *blood* on the screen for a superfast 1/50 of a second, no one would consciously see it. The viewers would, however, perceive the suggestive word subliminally. (*Sub-liminal* means *below the threshold* of awareness.) In this subconscious way, the audience would become more terrified watching the heroine's screaming close-up. They would not really know why, since they could not "see" the word *blood* dripping down star Cathy O'Donnell's face.

Since terror in any audience's head is an immeasurable variable, another experimenter interedited the movie *Picnic* not with *blood* but with *Drink Coca-Cola* and *Hungry? Eat Popcorn* at 1/3000 of a second every five seconds. Confection sales, unlike terror, are measurable. Because of the subliminal suggestions, the Coke sales at the Fort Lee, New Jersey, experimental moviehouse rose 57.7 percent and popcorn, 18.1 percent. Subliminals significantly swelled the sales.

In the late fifties, a radio station experimented with these Hidden Persuaders. The disc jockey announced that during the next song he would broadcast a message subliminal to the threshold of hearing. Listeners who could figure out what they couldn't hear were to call the station. What the jock broadcast was "Someone is at the door." One woman claimed that for the rest of the afternoon, "for some strange reason," she kept checking her front entrance as well as her drive-way. Another listener, later that night, woke suddenly from a deep sleep and knew exactly what subliminal message his subconscious had "heard" earlier in the day and had freed later into the swirl of his conscious dreams.

After a fashion, The Beatles subliminally engineered several of their albums: *Sgt. Pepper, Magical Mystery Tour,* and *Abbey Road*. Play these sides backwards, sideways, slow and fast, to get some idea not only of the hidden audibles but the deep-down subliminals John and Paul buried in the ninety-six tracks that make those albums so heavy. The mix of these subliminals was the start of the rumor that McCartney was dead.

Naturally, America took out after the subliminal Image Makers. You can't have people motivated by Hidden Persuaders, can you? What do you think of the morality of the Subliminal Sell? Subliminal persuading was ruled illegal. But is the illegal necessarily the immoral? Legality and morality are often two different things. Consider the possibilities.

Everyone agreed that Richard Nixon's TV image needed repair. What if the ad agency that filmed his TV campaign spots added words like *Patriotism, Motherhood, Apple Pie*. We couldn't see those words, but because Americans supposedly like patriotism, mothers, and apple pie, we would be subliminally influenced to transfer our goodwill to Mr. Nixon.

What if a rival agency removed Nixon's subliminals (sounds like a TV series plot, doesn't it?) and edited in instead 1/3000th pictures of nineteen-year-old dead soldiers, 1/50th word-flashes of *A-Bomb* or *High Taxes?* Would that be fair to Mr. Nixon?

Imagine a TV Eden of no conscious commercials. You'd no longer have, in the seven minutes between *Daniel Boone* and *Ironside*, thirty-seven different commercial spots before your eyes (including Station Identification). Instead the "unnoticeable" Subliminal Sell could make you want Fritos and Pepsi smack in the middle of David Brinkley's newscast, even though you loathe "junk food." Subliminal suggestion could barrage you with a hundred tension-making words, causing you a headache which other subliminals pushing aspirin and Bufferin could cure. It boggles the mind. What if Hitler had had it? Or what if now the Establishment or the new Revolutionaries should try it?

* * * *

The TV you watch at this point in 1971 revels in two basic sells: the Hard (Sock-it-to-'em) and the Soft (Sneak-it-to-'em).

About the Hard Sell nothing is subliminal. It blips on the screen shilling at you as if you were a moron, "proving" its products through demonstrations of slurping paper towels, invisible deodorant shields, and time-lapse photography that only numbskulls could believe. The Hard Sell is brassy, visually dull (e.g. some old guy sitting at a desk, pretending to be a doctor, pushing Nature's Remedy at you for your own good), and often offensive (like the Poli-Grip freak who digs his dentures into an apple and talks with his juicy mouth full telling you how his upper plate doesn't fall out of his face anymore).

So let Poli-Grip sue me.

After all, what is distasteful is, like beauty, in the mind of the beholder.

The King of Hard Sell Offensive was last year's Silva Thin cigarette commercials. Most of the Silva Thin spots built their "dramatic appeal" on a denigrating view of women. Witness: "Cigarettes are like women. The best ones are thin and rich." Small wonder Women's Lib has been screaming, "Up yours, Silva Thins!"

The Soft Sell commercial, on the other hand, is very like the subliminal in its indirect approach. The Soft Sell is a well photographed, pleasant package. You feel warm and beautiful watching the commercial come alive. The Soft-Sellers hope you will transfer your goodwill to their product. Xerox Corporation Super-Soft-Sells by withdrawing all interrupting commercials. They gentle you into their product by advertising only at the beginning and the end of the show.

Kodak is currently King of the Soft Touch.

Nice families, sunshine, and GI's coming back to their sweethearts to the tune of "The Green, Green Grass of Home" populate Kodak country. The outlawed Marlboro commercials, mythologized as superbly as they were photographed and edited, made you want to return to the honest simplicity of Marlboro Country. (Wherever *that* was.) Marlboro, you'll recall, never ever mentioned smoking. So Soft was their promise it almost said, if you can't say something good about smoking, don't say anything at all. Marlboro never really sold cigarettes. They sold real estate and an American myth of individual masculine freedom, wide as all outdoors.

TV has two other ways to suck you in: The Sex Sell and the Security Sell. (Either can be hard or soft.)

Sigmund Freud, the founder of psychoanalysis, theorized that everybody is motivated by sex. Madison Avenue calculates, therefore, that if you cast a beautiful "sister" in a car commercial, "dudes" will buy that car figuring she is standard equipment. The psychologist, Karen Horney, felt Freud was too narrow. More than by sex, she felt that people are motivated by security. In the Security Sell, "Mad Avenue" lays lines on you like:

"Don't be half-safe. Use Arrid to be sure."

"Ban won't wear off as the day wears on."

"Your social security number: Seagram's 7."

Pick up the point of all this? Once you understand critically how and why you react emotionally to commercials, you are no longer the TV brainwashers' victim. You get on top of the commercial psychology. You understand how companies try to manipulate you. You get to be an objective critic. And *voila*! You start seeing the TV commercial spots for the great little entertainments they are.

No matter what anyone says about *Myra Breckinridge*, author Gore Vidal's satire can hardly be faulted. Myra, talking of TV as the new high point of American culture, says:

> I must confess that I part company with Myron on the subject of TV. Even before Marshall McLuhan, I was drawn to the gray shadows of the cathode tube. In fact, I was sufficiently avant-garde in 1959

to recognize the fact that it was no longer the movies but the television commercial that engaged the passionate attention of the world's best artists and technicians. And now the result of their extraordinary artistry is this new world, like it or not, we are living in: post-Gutenberg and pre-Apocalypse. For almost twenty years the minds of our children have been filled with dreams that will stay with them forever, the way those maddening jingles do (as I write, I have begun softly to whistle "Rinso White," a theme far more meaningful culturally than all of Stravinsky or even John Cage…) The relationship between consumer and advertiser is the last demonstration of necessary love in the west, and its principal form of expression is the television commercial.

Vidal, using his Myra as a fictional cover for his long essay on American culture, argues well for the TV commercial as the New Art Form. Isn't it true in your own experience that the TV commercials are, more often than not, more enjoyable and intelligent than the shows they sponsor?

If money can buy the world's best artists and technicians, then why shouldn't the commercials be good? After all, a sixty-second commercial may be budgeted at $100,000 for that minute. What movie ever spread bread like that? (Two hours of *Easy Rider* cost only $400,000.) Since these TV persuaders cost so much, they must sell plenty. They must make us buy.

* * * *

The various commercial sells often overlap. New ones are constantly being invented. To the seven basic categories currently at the top of the TV marketeering, add your own nominees.

- THE SECURITY SELL. The basic appeal here, remember, is "conform to be safe." For example, three good-looking jocks repeat like sheep:

"I came back. I came back. I came back. To Brylcreem." "And we're glad they did," boops Betty the Cheerleader.

An adult-appeal variation of this is a pretense of doing your own thing within the confines of Establishment limits. You can "rebel" within the system: "The Dodge Rebellion wants you!" (Rebellion? Independence? Can you imagine the Black Panthers driving around in a Dodge?)

- THE SEX SELL. Seduction explains itself. Singer Lainie Kazan comes on like gangbusters for Aqua Velva after-shave: "I get a warm romantic notion, when you use Aqua Velva Lotion. That's how our romance began."

Then there's the Swedish girl who, over the music of "The Stripper," shills shaving lather: "Take it off. Take it all off."

If these are too latent, be blatant. Try: "New Ultra-Brite Toothpaste. The taste you can really feel…Gives your mouth. Whee! Ting! SEX APPEAL! "

- THE MUSICAL SELL. Done well, the musical commercial can be very pleasing; poorly conceived, nauseating. Beyond the jingle, the more sophisticated musical sell sometimes becomes a radio hit song in itself, like "Percolator," and Bob Crewe's original Pepsi theme: "Music to Watch Girls By."

Sometimes it borrows a song like the Schick Barber who sings "More" from the movie *Mondo Cane*, or the Marlboro Theme which is the title music from the cowboy movie *The Big Country*. Sometimes this Sell reaches us through satirical pop-culture nostalgia. Music hath indeed charms to soothe the savage buyer with its Soft soaping.

A-1 Sauce's Musical Sell glorifies the American Product like Ziegfield's *Follies* glorified the American Girl. While lovely ladies, dressed as national dishes from different countries, parade down a staircase past the camera, a voice-over announces grandly: "First there was salt and pepper and NOW (drum roll!) there is A-1 Sauce!"

Hollywood star Ann Miller condensed all the magic of MGM musicals for TV viewers with a one-minute extravaganza as she tapped away, with twenty chorus girls, in a big Busby Berkeley-like dance number for "Great American Soup."

Perhaps the jazziest Nostalgia Spot was the award-winning "Cold Diggers of 1969," a Contac commercial choreographed by TV's most famous dancer Peter Gennaro. Recalling, again, the ever-popular Busby Berkeley and his film *Gold Diggers of 1935*, twelve identically dressed chorines in identical blonde wigs tapped out the hit song, "Button up your overcoat when the wind blows free."

We have to laugh at the dancers' not-quite-precision routine. The exaggeration amuses us. What else can we do when our nose blows free, but remember to buy Contac.

- THE EGO-TRIP SELL. This is a variation of the Security Sell. We receive assurance we should do our own thing, and that we're beautiful, healthy, rich, and cool enough to do it.

Phillip Morris Filters assured us: "He's an independent guy."

Camel Filters told us: "Camel Filters. They're not for everybody."

Schlitz says, "You only go around once in life."

Clairol adds, "If I've only one life to live, let me live it as a blonde."

Virginia Slims cigarettes confirmed the femininity of liberated females with the frilly costumes backing up the line: "You've come a long way, Baby."

And Pepsi shores up our confidence by telling us: "You've got a lot to live."

- THE CATCH-PHRASE SELL. This seller makes his product name (or a punch-line from his product's commercial) into a household word.

Excedrin is the Catch-Phrase champion. Excedrin made "Mother, please. I'd rather do it myself!" into a nationwide joke. More recently, Excedrin has taught us that the superlative of headache is not "very *bad* headache," but is "I have an *Excedrin* headache."

Laugh-In's popularity is built on Catch Phrases. People feel they have to watch Rowan and Martin to be Up with the latest Catch to follow *bippy* and *sock-it-to-me*.

Get Smart added "Would you believe?" to our conversations. TV and its commercials change our language. And our grammar. Winston cigarettes advertised, "Winston tastes good like a cigarette should." Noting the difference between *like* and *as*, the very popular commercial added as a punch-line: "What do you want? Good grammar or good taste?"

- THE EPIC SELL. This relatively new genre imitating epic Hollywood movies gives you the impression that the grand product is larger than life.

Bacchus After-Shave enlists a cast of thousands to pull a huge flagon of Bacchus Lotion into a C. B. DeBiblical city. The thousand men become irresistible to their thousand wives. "At that moment, the Romans would march in and take over. And that," Bacchus' commercial insists, "is how the Romans conquered the world.... Go out and conquer your own empire."

Hai Karate, working the battle of the sexes in its epic punch-and-kick kung-fu commercials, makes even a quiet man so irresistible that the green bottle comes with a Self-Defense pamphlet to fight off women turned on by the cologne, warning, "The new Hai Karate after-shave is so powerful it drives women right out of their minds. Be careful how you use it."

This Epic genre is a huge Put-On, an exaggeration, spoken by an announcer whose tongue is planted hard in his cheek.

Seven Seas Salad Dressing sells Caesar Salad the same way. "Hail Caesar! Hail Caesar!" shouts the cast of Romans in togas.

- THE MAGIC SELL. The Wizardry Sell can be both the most inventive and the hardest to take.

Remember how "Wanda the Witch" started this sell for Hidden Magic Hairspray?

Remember Crest's "Decay Switch Witch" living in the bathroom medicine cabinet?

The "Giant Hand" in the washing machine?

The Ajax White Knight?

That Wizard of a Man from Glad?

The omens of the White Tornado and the Dove flying in the kitchen window?

Remember Manwich Sandwich for women who want to enchant husbands and children? Remember Latex Spred Paint for the time "when your house begins to haunt you"?

Remember the Giant Green Jolly?

If there be definition by example, these ample samples show you something about the Magic Sell. Historically, the Church and State tested witches to see if they were guilty or innocent.

Today on TV the tables are turned. The witch and sorcerer have become the testers and endorsers of every kind of wonderful and marvelous product. The advertising psychology is: If we can't prove this product through reason, you'll have to buy its magical results on faith alone.

* * * *

Television has programmed Americans into short attention spans. Sell it in twenty-five words or else don't sell it. Teachers met this problem when the first kids raised on TV hit kindergarten. Today, few young adults can bear to sit through a long old-style movie, much less a long concert or opera. We can enjoy Woodstock, the place, or *Woodstock*, the episodic movie, because we pay attention to it because we dig it.

Sesame Street, like *Laugh-In* requires an average twenty-second attention span. No one sits down to watch all of a program like *Sesame* or *Laugh-In* unless they were raised before TV and don't know any better. TV is not meant to be an Oberammergau Passion Play Marathon experience. Writers for TV scripts like *Judd for the Defense* peak their excitement every seven minutes: building to suspense right before each commercial.

The commercials themselves run thirty or sixty seconds. Of the primetime spots, eighty percent let it all out in thirty seconds. They sock the whole message to you: fast. The Great American Novel, all this considered, can no longer be predicted to be the Dostoyevskian length of *Gone with the Wind*. Broadway composers Jerome Ragni and James Rado may be right in their notes on the album of *Hair*. The narrative song called "Frank Mills"—less than twenty-five lines—is probably the Great American (Post-TV) Novel.

In our society, time is money. Americans, with hats off to the wild Oscar Wilde, know the price of everything and the value of very little. (That's perhaps the final difference between literal and metaphorical people.) Grant some inherent value to *The Movie of the Week*. That value you will find undercut by a TV Code maximum of ten minutes of commercials per primetime hour. Other times (mornings, afternoons, and late nights) the Code permits sixteen minutes of commercials an hour. So don't you ever pity Johnny Carson having to perform ninety minutes five nights a week. Nearly half of the Carson Show, forty minutes, is nothing but mass sell.

Should the willing suspension of disbelief you give *The Bold Ones* be broken by all these clarion calls to (under) arms? Is Pay-TV or Cable-TV the answer? Will the new videotape cassettes revolutionize programming so radically we will spend commercial-free evenings at home watching a rented video-cassette of a current Broadway hit musical like *The Rothschilds*?

For TV today, the Commercial Sell is the Frankenstein that creates our buffered, not-so-glad-wrapped, gotta-have-a-gimmick Americanned culture. Whenever business lays its hands on art, art suffers the slings and arrows of outrageous fortune hunters. If business exists to supply the demand, business often must create the demand. Advertisers, like politicians, tell us what they think we need, what they want us to demand, so they can supply it. In the following blank, enter your nominee for the most worthless product ever plugged as a necessity: _____ .

More complicated than shilling cornflakes, TV's real advertising potential comes not with selling *Products* but with selling *Attitudes*.

The critical viewer can hardly doubt it: check out the recent FCC ruling that the networks must give equal and free network time to responsible opponents of the President of the United States of America.

Times change and we change with them.

Ten years ago, Academy Award winner Joanne Woodward could not have publicly supported Planned Parenthood in a sixty-second plug about the Population Explosion.

Even if you cannot consider—along with the Dutch-Catholic theologians—that maybe the biblical dictum to multiply and fill the whole earth is ended now that the earth is SRO (standing room only), then you might consider the "Plurality of Opinion" that it is every person's duty to respect. After all, America, like love, is a many-splintered thing. TV, recognizing this of late, is now helping us get it together.

* * * *

Ever watch Sunday morning TV? Yech. Those so-called "religious" programs are often the worst kind of hard-sell. They are esthetically dull and intellectually insulting. The only thing worse than these Sunday "Holy Soaps" is the syndicated *Sermonette*, your local station's midnight sign-off—and turn-off—when it rolls short "inspirational" films of various depressing preachers tucking us into bed.

Dead, but not buried, such smug spirituality died in 1963 when super-satirist Stan Freberg slicked up the United Presbyterian Church with Soft-Sell inspiration. Religious commercials changed. Freberg's freestyle quickly inspired Los Angeles' St. Francis Productions. Their twenty-man Franciscan staff, budgeted at $150,000 annually, has found the Soft Spots of over seven hundred stations.

To knock those Sunday morning shows is not to knock religion. You needn't, after all, toss out the baby with the bathwater. The FCC requires each TV station to air a certain amount of public service programming. Freberg, the Franciscans, and your station figure alike: No one watches the doldrums of Sunday morning TV anyway, but prime-time viewers will catch a sixty-second spiritual ad slipped into an otherwise unsold commercial slot.

These spiritual commercials are more slick than sick. They're a sort of *Sesame Street* to teach adults about society. They focus on family, social, and political problems in easily digestible units. Friars Emery Tang and Karl Holtsnider of St. Francis Productions soft-sell street religion to everyday people. Sunday morning services are fine, say the Franciscans, but religion happens twenty-four hours a day. Franciscan scripts look like this:

Script No. 1
Scene: Cocktail party.
Situation: Host suggests playing a game of "Word Association."

HOST: Money.
GUESTS: Bills. Evil. Las Vegas.
HOST: Freeway.
GUESTS: Death. Ticket. Hurry.
HOST: God.
GUESTS: Dead silence. Stares.

As *Time* magazine points out: No one knows what to say about God anymore. Let's re-think Him.

Script No. 2
Scene: Close-up of Black hand shaking White hand. The hands hold.

VOICE-OVER:
All things considered, that's not very much is it?

Typical of their soft psyching, St. Francis Productions cool their Catholic viewpoint. They ecumenically emphasize the brotherhood of man and the unity of Christianity rather than Christian sectarianism.

Pope John XXIII would approve of the interchange ability of Catholic and Episcopal commercials.

One Episcopal plug dramatizes a middle-aged, middle-class, middle-western, mid-American flipping TV channels from one on-screen disaster to another. He finally tunes in a "Lions vs. Christians" movie.

The score as usual is "Lions, 406. Christians, 0."

Immediately he time-travels back into the Coliseum.

The VOICE-OVER says: "Being a Christian didn't use to be a spectator sport…It still isn't!"

* * * *

Besides selling "Religious" attitudes to this One Nation Indivisible ("under" the recently inserted "God"), TV commercials have been pressured to destroy socially harmful stereotypes and misconceptions rather than create them.

Italians dislike the Mafia names used on detective shows like *The FBI*. Jay Silverheels, playing Tonto as sidekick to the Lone Ranger, insists he is not the last of the Mohicans. Like Cree singer Buffy St. Marie, Silverheels campaigns for "real" Indians to play "reel" Indians. If palefaces must portray Indians, Silverheels wishes them to act with greater dignity. Madison Avenue is learning not to ask Silverheels to be typecast as a sidekick to another TV hero dressed in white: the Man from Glad. How's that grab your greater dignity?

Even when the stereotype is "humorous," offense can be taken. Chicanos have protested the Frito Bandito out of television existence.

Stereotypes, no matter how "humorous," says Dr. Kenneth B. Clark, professor of psychology at New York City College, "almost invariably assert the inferiority of one group and the superiority of another. Needless to say, these explanations are satisfying to the group on top, and disturbing to the group on the bottom."

The ad agencies have long celebrated the narrow Judaeo-WASP stereotypes of beauty, humor, and superiority. But as Peggy Lee sings, "Is that all there is?" Emphatically no!

New agencies, like Manhattan's Zebra, have succeeded in the last two years on their premise that "Integrated Is Also Beautiful." Co-racial to the proportion its name implies, Zebra's Black management is a far cry from the Black ad men that film-maker Robert Downey created in his satire on ad agencies, race, and corporate power, *Putney Swope*. The movie itself is in black-and-white, except for the TV commercials the agency shoots in color.

Zebra's advertising promotes alternative standards of beauty, behavior, and popular culture. Aren't we all freer for no longer having to be Clairol blondes or WASP Brylcreem jocks?

Chicago's "Project Straight Dope" destroys misconceptions and sells reality in its anti-drug abuse campaign. Straight Dope's short spots are cold and reasoned. Steve Lehner, vice-president and creative supervisor of North Advertising, explained Straight Dope's commercials to *Chicago Sun- Times*' Ron Powers:

> The spots are terse. Stark. They are terribly honest. Unslick. Real. The intrusive sound of a Moog synthesizer is the attention-getter. An un-announcer voice achieves the one-to-one relationship with the listener. He presents the facts coldly and precisely. He explains why dope is dumb. He gives the listener the tools he needs to say no to narcotics.
>
> The ads are designed to make kids think for themselves. This is not easy because kids are not introduced to narcotics by a gangster in a trench coat. Kids are introduced to narcotics by their friends. It is hard to say no to a friend.

Beyond such a public-service Reality Pitch, and Nearer-My-Cash-to-Thee, is the Commercial of Golly-Gee-Whiz Verisimilitude.

You know: the lady caught by the candid camera in her favorite laundromat, the man who endorses his favorite product in a parking lot. Since nothing succeeds like *reality* these frank days, commercial film-makers like Chicago's young Michael Gray often prefer the total reality of an actual location to a studio set. With today's lightweight equipment, Gray finds no need to shoot anywhere but the actual site, whether filming an old-timey pub for a *Chicago Tribune* TV spot or shooting in Kentucky for Colonel Sanders.

Real locations require real people. Put yourself in the shoes of young California housewife Sue Sherwood. She read a small ad in her local newspaper: "Mother, would you like to participate in a household experiment? We'll pay baby-sitting and transportation." She made contact and was told to ask no *Mission Impossible* questions. Her instructions told her to bundle her dirty laundry and take it to a motel. She was interviewed, taken to a laundromat, given soap for her wash, and told if she was caught or killed the *Mission* staff would disavow any knowledge of her existence.

So far so good. Then enter Rose Marie, co-star of *The Dick Van Dyke Show* and *The Doris Day Show*. Rosie made pleasant enough conversation about kids, families, detergents, and then laid it on Mrs. Sherwood: "Do you know you've been on TV all along?" If the screeching Mrs. Sherwood didn't, she did the day Tide rewarded her 4,000 dollars for spontaneously endorsing their product.

Mrs. Sherwood lived the American Dream: she got something for nothing.

Not many have her luck.

Even with a portfolio of composites (glossy photos of oneself) and a resume (of modeling, acting, or technical experience), the competition is keen even for brothers and sisters who can get it all on.

As of 1971, nearly seven hundred non-entertainment production companies, varying in size from three to a hundred people, telefilm 15,000 different gigs annually. These include films for company training-via-videotape, public relations, sports, technical and scientific information. (Cape Kennedy launches, for instance, are photographed by as many as eighty technical cameras.) In the US approximately 115,000 men and women produce TV commercials and spot announcements for national, regional, and local distribution. Searching for a career? The field is wide-open and growing, growing, growing.

OLD STEREOTYPES
NEW MYTHS

Vaudeville is not dead. It's alive and well on TV. It's sponsored. Ed Sullivan proves it. As vaudeville once was America's major folk entertainment, Sullivan and the sub-Sullivan TV shows that ape his variety make it happen for the widest possible cross-section of America. Some people watch some of the shows some of the time, and some of the people watch some of the shows none of the time; but sooner or later everyone, as proved in the musical *Bye Bye Birdie*, watches Ed Sullivan.

Sullivan's variety mixes his audience. Youngsters tune in to watch Neil Diamond and catch a scene from *Man of La Mancha*. Oldsters tune in to see how Fred Astaire or some other old timey star is holding up, and they stay to watch Creedence Clearwater Revival. On Sullivan, everybody ends up being exposed to things they wouldn't necessarily choose to watch: like, especially, Swiss Bell Ringers and Yugoslavian bear acts.

When The Beatles sang "Let It Be" for Sullivan, however, some of those exposed went up in arms over McCartney writing the lyric "Mother Mary comes to me." Sullivan received national mail, and local radio stations banned the song. The conservative gripe: no rock group should take the name of Mary in vain; Christ's mother deserves respect. When lyricist Paul McCartney revealed that his own mother's name was Mary, the stations over-ruled the prescriptive censors and the song has become a Beatles classic.

TV is a mass medium. If a 45-rpm record is a million seller, the rock group is a success. If a TV show attracts a million viewers, the network bounces it off the air. TV talks in terms of fifty million viewers a night, watching one hundred million dollars of commercials pushing mass-produced products.

TV influences, in program and promotion, the collective mass mind.

Of the estimated 213 million television sets in the world, about 78 million are in the United States. The Soviets have 25 million; the Japanese, 20.5 million; and the United Kingdom, 19 million. TV helps make you who you are.

And when TV *talks* about successful format and surefire formula, TV *means* that stereotyped characters without personality and stereotyped situations without depth are easiest for the mass audience attracted to the small screen. TV gauges its average program level to the twelve-year-old viewer. Does TV underestimate its viewers' capacity? Are idiotic game shows like *The Dating Game* and nitwitted situation comedies like *The Beverly Hillbillies* really necessary?

Consider the success of that sitcom formula we'll call "Daddy Is a Dummy." Through many TV seasons sitcom husbands like Blondie's Dagwood, Harriet's Ozzie, Lucy's Ricky, and Mary Tyler Moore's Dick Van Dyke bumbled and puzzled their way through situations which only the wife could solve. Talk about Women's Lib! Many recent shows have done away with Daddy altogether: *The Lucy Show, Doris Day,* and *Julia.* Seems these merry widows can't say anything nice about Daddy, so they don't say anything at all.

On the other hand, Mothers have gotten the same boot. *My Three Sons* went motherless for years. *Family Affair* is held together by a dirty old man. John Forsyth's *To Rome With Love* is an Italian version of his previous series *Bachelor Father.* If stereotypes are a clue to where the mass mind is, then American psychology is preoccupied—no matter how comic TV makes it—with broken homes.

But are homes broken by death, divorce, or disappearance some fearful new plague caused by TV? Of course not! Critics too often look for cause and effect where cause and effect is a puppy chasing its own tail.

Can you say TV violence is the cause of violence in the streets? For years we have had situation comedy on TV and we have never had situation comedy in the streets. If anything, society is the cause of television. It is within the mass medium of TV that our mass mind surfaces with our mass preoccupations.

MASS MIND
STEREOTYPE
ARCHETYPE

Psychologist Carl Jung claims some experiences are true for all people at all times. We all remember our individual life-experiences. Actor Lee Marvin, for one, claims he can remember the wombtime before he was born. Jung contends that besides our personal memories we each participate in the Collective Memory of Mankind.

As each one of us unconsciously remembers our personal birth, so, says Jung, does the Collective Unconscious of collective mankind remember the human race crawling up from the evolutionary sea into creation on the shore. Perhaps Jung's theory explains why the ocean can hypnotize us into hours of staring. Our Collective Unconscious is reliving faint echoes of that time of collective birth.

Fairy tales, Jung says, because they are composed and retold over long periods of time by many different people, reflect collective patterns of human attitudes toward family, parents, brothers, sisters, guilt, and security. The Bible stories of Cain and Abel with Adam and Eve—while finally written down—were, according to the most modern scriptural exegesis, originally folk tales which—if Jung were consulted—would likewise measure the collective hopes and fears of the people who heard and modified and told them.

Today the folktale and fairy tale, like the classical tales of Greece and Rome, are still being told. But this time, instead of around the nomadic campfire or the medieval hearth, they occur as television tales.

TV is the folk-medium of our time.

Jung saw patterns emerging in folk and fairy tales. He called these constant repetitions *archetypes*. These archetypes included basic *plots*, basic *characters*, basic *places*, and basic *things* common to all human experience. In America, the TV-movie Western is a basic archetypal plot that has been around since before Good confronted Evil in the medieval morality plays.

President Nixon, whose favorite star is John Wayne, has wondered publicly, "Why it is that the Westerns survive year after year with such popularity. Although this may be a square observation," the President continued, "it may be because of the satisfying moral structure of the Western as an art form: the good guys come out ahead, the bad guys lose, and there is no question about who is to be admired."

The Western has long been established as a TV staple.

The *Bonanza* format of a Good-Guy Family fighting not to be dispossessed of their land has been repeated constantly in *The High Chaparral*, *The Big Valley* (wherein a Mother, Barbara Stanwyck, replaced the Father, Lorne Greene of *Bonanza*), and *The Men from Shiloh* (aka *The Virginian*). The archetypal plot here is Adam fighting not to be driven off his property in Eden. The updated version of the Western is the police-detective series like *Hawaii Five-O* where Good Guys battle to save the Eden of their tropical paradise from Bad Guys.

TV's attitudes are often contradictory. Still they are no more ambivalent, program to program, than the multiple myths which feed into our TV literature. In the Western, for instance, the raw land is considered good. The West is as much an Eden as Marlboro Country. When somebody from a Western goes "back East" or "off to the city," chances are he or she will be ruined. The city is considered an evil place. On the other hand, the city is often the best of all possible worlds. Just ask *That Girl!* (Christianity, since its beginnings, has, by the way, always been an urban phenomenon. St. Paul traveled city to city; and Augustine wrote of "The City of God.")

Sometimes, the myth of the country meets the myth of the city, so a cowboy-in-the-city TV series like *McCloud* is born. In New York City this last autumn, at the west end of 42nd Street, facing toward Times Square was a gigantic Marlboro billboard. Starting at the fifth story, the Marlboro Man lighted his cigarette in his cupped hands. Tall in the saddle, he stretched all the way up to the eleventh floor. Six—count 'em—six stories of rawhide male, smack in the heart of America's largest city, saying, "Come to Marlboro Country." In *McCloud*, TV's version of the Oscar-winning movie *Midnight Cowboy*, the myth of the West moves in on the myth of the city. It is no sudden accident of American psychic history that detective McCloud walks 42nd Street dressed as a Marlboro Man. Riding in from the West, he is the Good Guy come to save the city from crime and pollution.

And every social worker knows, the East needs saving. Ever since James Fenimore Cooper's Leatherstocking frontiersman Natty Bumppo fled the East, Americans' salvation has lain in the West. John Steinbeck's family of Joads in *The Grapes of Wrath* migrated West to California—the Promised Land. "Go West, young man," Horace Greeley said, and go West they did. All except F. Scott Fitzgerald's not-so-great

Gatsby who went East to seek his fortune and paid with his life for living *East of Eden.* The very Journey West has become an American myth in itself. (Didn't the Mamas and Papas sing the lure of "California Dreamin'" and didn't the Beach Boys "Wish They All Could Be California Girls"?) It is significant that motorcycling East on their road trip across America, Peter Fonda and Dennis Hopper were murdered for, thematically, journeying in the wrong direction!

The archetype opposite to the man who retains his Eden through true grit is, obviously, the man dispossessed of one Eden and in search of another.

A constant TV hero is the traveling cowpoke, whether he travels by traditional horseback, by motorcycle (*Then Came Bronson*), or by car (*Follow the Sun, Route 66*). Sometimes this man who is "looking for something" is as vague as Ben Gazzara in *Run for Your Life* or Patrick MacGoohan in *The Prisoner.* What these restless and pursued men have in common is their dispossession from Eden.

* * * *

It is archetypally true that no human likes to blame himself. Adam blamed Eve. Eve blamed the serpent. Cain blamed Abel. Our small-screen TV heroes, like the mythical heroes of old, fix the blame for their guilt or dispossession wherever they can: on people, places, things. Black comedian Flip Wilson says it for all of us: "The Devil made me do it!" The Devil, however, is long gone. In his place now stand many alternative archetypes.

* * * *

"A woman is a sometime thing." So George Gershwin wrote in the archetypal American musical, *Porgy and Bess.* In how many fairy tales (and how many novels, plays, and telefilms) does the Archetypal Evil Stepmother replace the dead

Archetypal Good Mother? In "Let It Be," is The Beatles' Mother Mary much different from Cinderella's Fairy Godmother or Dorothy's White Witch in Oz? Like *Bewitched*'s Samantha or the mothers in *The Partridge Family* (based on the musical group, The Cowsills) and *The Brady Bunch*, these ladies come in time of trouble to help. Just like Donna Reed used to in the 1950s.

The Good Women are the opposite of those Evil Women who plague not only Hansel and Gretel but also the likes of the heroes who have troubles with ladies on *The Name of the Game* or *Bracken's World*. To test the application of this archetype to you, confess: Every one of you reading this has been, at one time or another, so angry at your mother that you knew you had to be an adopted child. Your real mother could never treat you like this.

* * * *

Parents and other strangers. In his revolutionary book, *Do It*, required reading in many universities, author Jerry Rubin writes, "You've got to kill your parents."

Literal people who believe "one *only* equals one" immediately miss his metaphor.

The archetypal myth behind such an extreme generation gap rarely leads to a hack job like Lizzie Borden's. But there is a rebellious bit of Lizzie in every child. Or there should be. Your parents need to "die" to you as parents if you're ever to become independent and if they're ever to become your friends. Once you're older isn't it true you don't really need them as parents, and can better do with them as wise friends?

Be that as it may, the ancient Greek expression of this had Oedipus killing his father, ruining his mother's life, and blinding himself. In another classical myth, Telemachus was fated to search for his father Ulysses. This is the same archetypal plot as Johnny Cash singing as a father on TV about "A Boy Named Sue" or Walter Brennan's old series, *The Guns of Will Sonnett*. Will Sonnett combined the archetypal place of the West with this archetype of the missing father who must be tracked down by his son.

Ever since Adam glommed down on Cain for killing Abel, the three males with their wife and mother Eve have served as the Archetypal Family. Soap operas like *The Secret Storm* pick up on this intra-family turmoil. The fact that millions of viewers watch the soaps each afternoon indicates a common enough chord is struck to label Family Turmoil as an archetype. To get a look at this Family Turmoil Pattern—without the dulling Soap film—try Eugene O'Neill's *Long Day's Journey into Night* and Edward Albee's *American Dream* or *Who's Afraid of Virginia Woolf*. Then add a little *Romeo and Juliet*, a little *Lion in Winter*, and a little *Death of a Salesman*.

* * * *

Stereotypes differ from archetypes. Archetypes are the nitty-gritty essence of persons, places, or things that everyone who has ever lived has to some degree or another deeply experienced: like birth, fear of death, guilt, love, sex, anguish, and so on. Stereotypes, on the other hand, don't run so deep. Stereotypes are shallow siphonings off the top of archetypes. An archetype conjures the essence. The stereotype settles for the easy surface, the facile generalization. Bernard Malamud's novel and due-for-TV film, *The Fixer*, plunges deep into the guts of the archetypal suffering Jew. Shakespeare's *Merchant of Venice* deals somewhat with the superficial stereotype of the Jewish protagonist as a shrewd businessman.

Hollywood in the seventies is more famous for its Television City Studios than it ever was for MGM. More TV shows than movies are currently shot in the former film capital of the world. Yet Hollywood, from the old movies like *Birth of a Nation* (1915) up until this latest TV season, has more often than not settled for the easy stereotype, the laugh-getting racism.

In the thirties all Hollywood Negroes, like Stepin Fetchit and Rochester, had "rhythm," were lazy, and afraid of ghosts. Would Butterfly McQueen, Scarlett's black maid in *Gone with the Wind*, be possible in 1971? By the end of the sixties, Hollywood was into a new stereotype. Blacks became "noble." Male and female Hollywood created them. They could do no wrong. The handsome Sidney Poitier rose to stardom with the rise of this limited stereotype. This TV season stereotype has evolved into more realistic presentations of Black people on screen. Over sixteen series currently feature Blacks in more dimensioned roles than ever before.

In Chicago, Black filmmaker Melvin Van Peebles, director of last year's controversial racial movie, *Watermelon Man*, has a new film creating a new kind of liberated Black protagonist—who is no sidekick or servant—starring in a provocative movie whose title explains itself: *Sweet Sweetback's Baadasssss Song.*

Such an array of Black talent in human roles on big and small screens means, we all hope, the final demise of the Negro stereotype. The only Negro with rhythm among this season's performers tap dances Saturday nights on the reactionary *Lawrence Welk Show.* Welk dedicates his variety hour to telling it like it isn't about race, college, and life in our American cities.

Black Professor John Oliver Killens of Columbia University reported to *TV Guide* the criticism of Black TV shows made by a blue-collar Black man: "Ain't no Black shows. They're just shows with Black people acting like they White."

One of Killens' students in a Black Culture class said: "That cat in *Mission: Impossible* is the natural end. He's the White folks' handyman. They should call that show *I*

Was a Stooge for the CIA. Nevertheless, Blacks are no longer invisible men on the small screen. (Read Ralph Ellison's *Invisible Man*.) The Negro has surfaced in the seventies in as many roles as are—despite racial controversies—humanly possible.

The objection to *Mission: Impossible*'s Greg Morris, although debatable, is right on the difference between stereotype and archetype. To begin with, Morris' skills are dramatically depicted as being technically way beyond those of a mere "handyman." Secondly, he fits into the Jonathan-David Archetype. Jonathan befriending King David is archetype opposite to Cain killing Abel.

Older even than the Bible story, this archetype of two men in partnership recurs repeatedly. In "modern" literature, the seventeenth-century Cervantes' "Man of La Mancha," Don Quixote, rode with Sancho Panza. More recently, the Cisco Kid had Pancho, the Lone Ranger had Tonto, *The Mod Squad* had Clarence Williams in a *Three Musketeers* variation. Remember the outsider, d'Artagnan, the fourth Musketeer, who joins up to bond with the original Three?

These cross-racial partnerships grow directly out of Fenimore Cooper's American tradition. In frontier times, Leatherstocking had his faithful equal, the Indian Chingachgook. Is—as Killens' student implies—this Jonathan-David Archetype necessarily demeaning to one of the partners?

Joe Buck in *Midnight Cowboy* had Ratso Rizzo.

Dragnet's Sergeant Friday has his Gannon.

Adam 12's veteran Molloy has his rookie Reed.

* * * *

William Ross Wallace, in the nineteenth century paid tribute to Woman Power with "The hand that rocks the cradle is the hand that rules the world."

In the twentieth-century teleconomy, the hand that pays the bills is the hand that rules the networks. A recent magazine advertisement for "Sponsor Power" belonged to General Telephone and Electronics:

> We own Sylvania TV.
>
> We're worried about some of the shows you see on your sets.
>
> It's not enough for us just to make good TV sets. We also want to make sure you get...good, tasteful, intelligent shows on them. For a purely selfish reason: we want to keep you from being turned off to TV. Our sponsoring of quality shows like *CBS Playhouse* is not enough. We believe that the shows shouldn't be hacked to bits by "a few words from the sponsor." We don't interrupt any of our specials with commercials.

Now *that* sounds like a responsible sponsor. Most network programmers and advertisers stand guilty as accused by *TV Guide* of "contempt for the American public." Do as many top network executives, as Triangle intimates, admit their primetime programs are trash? Do as many advertising executives buy time on programs they know are trivia? Generally speaking, it's those Nielsen Ratings that convince networks and advertisers of what the public wants.

Arthur C. Nielsen's company, a market-research firm, spends less than fifty percent of its time on Nielsen's infamous *TV Index*. A low Nielsen rating can axe a network show no matter what the critics say, or how a good percentage of the viewers feel. Nielsen's *TV Index* scores how many families and what types of viewers are reached by sales pitches at any given minute. There's no point in Playtex Living Gloves ("Glamorous Housework Gloves for lovelier hands in just nine days") sponsoring the *Monday Night NFL Game*.

Nielsen's yardstick is important to sponsors paying a primetime minimum of $15,000 to $20,000 a minute; and up to $140,000 per minute for consistent Nielsen topper, *The Bob Hope Show*. The terror of the Nielsen rating is the constant American terror of quantity over quality. Neither Nielsen nor the sponsor asks how good is the show, or how much do viewers enjoy it. The ratings exploit only: How much can be sold how fast to how many.

Nielsen claims a scientific cross-selection of American homes for his projections. His electronic Audimeter, attached to these "representative" home receivers, reads once a minute the channels viewed in each sample home. Nielsen projects on a premise long used by newspapers, magazines, and radio: for every letter received, pro or con, there are at least ten readers or listeners who haven't bothered to write. Ten letters equal the opinions of one hundred people.

Nielsen's spread of Audimeters connects by telephone cables to computers at the Nielsen home center in Chicago. Sponsors can know immediately how many viewers have seen their commercial.

There is a flaw in Nielsen's ointment, however. Nielsen services businessmen, and businessmen are notorious for their resistance to new ideas.

The TV that hit the US in 1947 is not the TV of 1971. TV, like all else, evolves. Viewers have assimilated the TV set into their total environment. The businessmen have not caught the new pace. Their nineteen-forties' sensibilities have not re-conceptualized TV into its seventies' role. They cannot believe that not all viewers still sit deliberately in front of their TV sets the way families gathered around the tube to set endurance records in 1951.

They cannot understand the changing sculptural quality of the TV set itself in the aftermath of nineteen-sixties psychedelia. How many young viewers turn off the sound, distort the color intensity, and put the picture into a horizontal roll while they listen to hard-rock albums on their stereo record players.

Does business really not realize that the American tribe has taken the TV set to its archetypal heart?

We gather around the TV the way we once gathered around the colonial hearth and the western campfire. We gather round and watch re-tellings of the old stories of life and love and death. We sit on the floor and mourn the deaths of Kings and Kennedys: Martin, Jack, and Bobby.

Often, too, we switch on the electronic sculpture of the TV set and more or less ignore it, the way we hang a painting in the livingroom: mostly to glance at it, and to study only occasionally.

* * *

Little children, as usual, lead the way. The TV set has been part of kids' environment since infancy. They play all morning in front of the twenty-four-inch screen inadvertently hearing sound and seeing picture. They give the set attention only when it interests them. They play before it like children before a hearthfire, hardly conscious of its presence until it is desired like food or warmth, information or entertainment.

Primitive peoples, living close to their archetypes, build shrines in their dwellings for their gods and totems. The TV set is the American shrine. Around it we hear vague reminders of the old myths. TV technology is the latest re-telling of the old archetypal truths we deep down so much like to re-hear.

Re-imagine the TV set.

Don't condemn it because businessmen make it less than it could be. Plenty of good vibes happen in this most encyclopedic and educational of all media. Be critical, but relax into its possibilities.

Think Jung!

As Good Mother Mary counsels, "Let it be."
Let it happen.

REFLECTIONS

STUDY GUIDE
CLASSROOM DISCUSSION
AND
HOW TO MAKE YOUR OWN MOVIE

Reflections in a Golden Eye

1. What is the value of criticism? Why does television viewing demand a critical audience?

2. What is a "metaphor"? Does having a metaphorical mind enable the viewer to appreciate TV more fully?

3. Would Thoreau consider television a "pretty toy"? Is it something much more than this?

4. How is TV like an eye? Is it golden?

5. What effect has the invention of television had on traditional education? Have educational methods changed much since the inception of TV?

6. "Would our society be better for watching late-night videotapes...of the trial of the Chicago Seven? Of Charles Manson? Of Lt. Calley?"

7. How does the fact of television censorship challenge the American guarantee of free speech and free press?

8. What is the difference between "descriptive" and "prescriptive" censorship? Would you favor "open TV" or "censored TV"?

9. Why doesn't South Africa have national television?

10. What role does TV play in politics?

Afternoon at the Soap Opera

1. Do you agree that the soap opera is "denial, masochistic, narcotic"? How did the actual cast feel about *The Secret Storm*?

TV's Queasy Kid Stuff

1. Why is *Sesame Street* so appealing to children?

2. What is the "Dagwood Syndrome"? Does exposing children to stupid TV males and spineless fathers alter their respect for paternal intellect and authority?

3. What should parents do about the distorted images of men and women that their children are exposed to on television?

Americanned Creativity

1. Does subliminal advertising on TV exist? If so, is it immoral? Illegal?

2. What is the "Hard Sell"? What do you think is the most offensive "Hard Sell" on TV today?

3. Is Gore Vidal's assessment of the TV commercial correct? Are commercials "more often than not more enjoyable and intelligent than the bummer shows they sponsor"?

4. Give examples of commercials which can be classified as: "Security Sell"; "Sex Sell"; "Musical Sell"; "Ego-trip Sell";

"Catch-phrase Sell"; "Epic Sell"; and "Magic Sell." Why is it important to understand TV advertising techniques such as these?

5. What kinds of attitudes does TV sell?

Old Stereotypes, New Myths

1. What is a "stereotype"? What are some of the stereotypes created by TV?

2. Does TV reflect our culture accurately and completely? Is it the twentieth-century "folk-medium"?

3. What is an "archetype"? Do you agree that TV employs classical archetypes in its dramas, comedies and Westerns? Is the comparison too far-out?

4. Name two recent TV shows which use the Good Woman and the Evil Woman archetypes.

5. What criticism does this text level at the current shows which feature Black performers?

6. What is the drawback of the Nielsen rating system?

7. What innovations must tele-planners make so that TV will become a more meaningful expression in our culture?

Projection Project

SHOOT YOUR OWN MOVIE!
On Your Own, or as a Class Project

A basic premise of film and TV viewing is, once you've gotten behind a camera your perception and appreciation of the art of television increases. So, sharpen your critical ability.

For less than two dollars, two (or more) people can share three minutes of fifty feet of 8 or Super-8 color movie film. Buy Anscochrome II or Dynacolor movie film. Both are cheap and processing is included.

Borrow a camera or recruit a group of four or five, and rent a Super-8 from your local photo shop. (Around four dollars.) You can take turns shooting, helping, and learning from one another. Make five commercials, or work together as a production crew on one sixty-second spot. You'll be surprised that the shorter a commercial is, the more salient a punch it needs.

SUGGESTIONS
FILMMAKING 101

1. Decide on your product, theme, or message. Decide the kind of Sell you want. Maybe you'll try for a Hard Sell to gain an appreciation of that particular form. Use a 45-rpm record, street sounds on tape, or a recording of the TV news. Write your own catch-phrase dialogue.

2. Before filming people, experiment shooting a few magazine pictures close up. If you have no flood lamps, improvise with sunlight through a window. Decide how long you want each image on screen. Super-8 shows eighteen frames per second.

3. If your camera has a zoom lens, zoom in or out from a part of the picture to the whole. If shooting real-life action, don't pan the camera (move it from side-to-side in a sweeping motion) too fast.

4. Editing. When the three minutes of raw footage returns from the processor, the fun begins. Buy a package of editing tape. It costs only a few cents. Using either an editing machine or a straight fingernail scissors, cut out the bad sequences and splice together the good in the proper order.

5. When your film is complete, project it on a screen, or on a wall, playing your 45-rpm record or your tapes as your soundtrack on another machine.

If you solo, you'll bear the whole creative burden, all the success or all the failure. Maybe you work best that way. In a group production, however, you have obvious advantages.

Different strokes for different folks, right?

Some of your crew may specialize in one phase of production, depending on your needs: writing, direction, camera, editing, lighting, animation, titles, sound recording, set decoration, costuming.

Small crews often double in the usual professional combinations of writer-director, director-editor, cameraman-editor, cameraman-soundman. The combos are as varied as your talents, interests, and ambitions.

www.ingramcontent.com/pod-product-compliance
Lightning Source LLC
Chambersburg PA
CBHW021122080526
44587CB00010B/602